Career Planning

for Teens

A Comprehensive Guide to Essential Skills for Career Exploration and Development to Prepare for the Job Market in the Digital Age

Isabella Wells

© 2024 by Isabella Wells

All rights reserved. No part of this book may be reproduced or transmitted in any form or by any means, electronic or mechanical, including photocopying, recording, or by any information storage and retrieval system, without written permission from the author, except for the inclusion of brief quotations in a critical review.

As a seasoned career counselor, I've witnessed firsthand the transformative power of informed career planning. In this guide, tailored specifically for teens, I draw upon years of experience to provide comprehensive advice and practical strategies for navigating the ever-evolving job market. My aim is to empower young readers with the essential skills they need to explore potential career paths, set achievable goals, and thrive in the digital age workforce. Let's embark on this journey of self-discovery and professional growth together.

Isabella Wells

Contents

Introduction — 7

Chapter One — 13
Discovering Your Passion and Purpose — 13
   Exploring Your Interests and Values — 13
   Identifying Your Unique Strengths and Talents — 16
   Finding Inspiration: Role Models and Success Stories — 19

Chapter Two — 23
Navigating the Modern Career Landscape — 23
   Traditional vs. Non-Traditional Career Paths — 23
   Future-Proof Jobs and Emerging Trends — 27
   Entrepreneurship and Side Hustles for Teens — 32

Chapter Three — 37
Setting SMART Career Goals — 37
   Short-term and Long-term Goal Setting — 37
   Creating a Personalized Career Roadmap — 41

Overcoming Obstacles and Staying Motivated 45

Chapter Four   **51**

Developing Essential Skills for Success   **51**

    Communication and Interpersonal Skills   51

    Critical Thinking and Problem-Solving   55

    Time Management and Productivity Hacks   60

Chapter Five   **65**

Gaining Real-World Experience   **65**

    Internships and Apprenticeships 101   65

    Volunteering and Community Involvement   71

    Starting a Business or Side Gig   75

Chapter Six   **81**

Acing Academics and Extracurriculars   **81**

    Balancing School, Activities, and Career Prep   81

    Choosing the Right Educational Path   87

    Navigating College Applications and Finances   91

Chapter Seven   **97**

Building Your Personal Brand   **97**

    Creating an Online Portfolio and Presence   97

Networking and Making Connections — 101

Developing Confidence and Self-Marketing Skills — 106

Chapter Eight — 113
Job Search and Interview Mastery — 113

Crafting Winning Resumes and Cover Letters — 113

Acing Job Interviews and Following Up — 118

Exploring Alternative Job Search Strategies — 123

Chapter Nine — 129
Embracing Diversity and Inclusion — 129

Overcoming Challenges and Stereotypes — 129

Celebrating Diverse Backgrounds and Perspectives — 132

Creating an Inclusive Career Plan — 136

Chapter Ten — 141
Lifelong Learning and Adaptability — 141

Developing a Growth Mindset — 141

Continuous Learning and Skill Development — 144

Pivoting and Reinventing Your Career — 148

Exclusive Bonus   **153**

    20 of the most profitable occupations in the digital era   153

Introduction

In the ever-evolving and increasingly competitive job market, embarking on the journey of career planning can feel like navigating a labyrinth of choices, uncertainties, and self-discovery. As a seasoned career counselor, I've had the privilege of guiding countless individuals through this transformative process, witnessing firsthand the power of purposeful planning and strategic decision-making.

Allow me to share a story that encapsulates the profound impact career planning can have on one's life. It was a crisp autumn morning when Sarah, a bright-eyed high school senior, walked into my office, her backpack laden with dreams and apprehensions. Like many teens, she felt overwhelmed by the multitude of career paths before her, unsure of where to begin.

Our initial conversations revealed a young woman with a passion for art and a deep desire to make a positive impact on the world. However, societal pressures and self-doubt had clouded her vision, causing her to question her aspirations. It was then that we embarked on a transformative journey, delving into the realms of self-discovery, goal-setting, and strategic planning.

Through a series of interactive exercises and honest conversations, Sarah unearthed her innate strengths, values, and unique talents. We explored unconventional career paths, blending her artistic flair with her commitment to social change. Slowly but surely, her confidence began to soar, and a clear vision emerged – to become a socially-conscious graphic designer, using her creativity to amplify important causes and inspire positive change.

With a renewed sense of purpose, Sarah crafted a personalized career roadmap, outlining milestones, skill development opportunities, and networking strategies. She dove headfirst into extracurricular activities, internships, and portfolio-building projects, each step bringing her closer to her dream.

Today, Sarah is a thriving graphic designer, working with non-profit organizations and social enterprises, using her art to create powerful visual narratives that drive impact. Her journey is a testament to the power of career planning – a process that not only illuminates potential pathways but also fosters self-awareness, resilience, and the courage to blaze one's trail.

As you embark on your career planning adventure, this book will serve as your trusted companion, guiding you through a comprehensive exploration of self-discovery, goal-setting, skill development, and strategic decision-making. Together, we will navigate the complexities of the modern job market, uncover your unique strengths and passions, and chart a course toward a fulfilling and rewarding career.

Whether you're a high school student brimming with curiosity, a college student seeking direction, or a young professional contemplating a career transition, this book will empower you to take charge of your professional journey. Through engaging narratives, practical exercises, and expert insights, you'll learn to embrace a growth mindset, cultivate essential skills, and develop the adaptability to thrive in an ever-changing landscape.

Prepare to embark on a transformative journey of self-discovery, where you'll unearth your true potential and gain the confidence to pursue your dreams fearlessly. Together, we'll unlock the secrets to crafting a rewarding and meaningful career – one that aligns with your values, ignites your passion and leaves a lasting impact on the world around you.

So, take a deep breath, open your mind, and get ready to unleash the power of career planning. Your future awaits, and the path to success starts here.

Chapter One

Discovering Your Passion and Purpose

Exploring Your Interests and Values

Before you can begin to plan your career effectively, you must first identify your interests and values. To choose a career that you love and is purposeful for you, it is important to think about what makes you happy and fulfilled.

Your interests are the things that pique your curiosity and make you happy. They fall into many different categories, including artistic, scientific, entrepreneurial, and athletic. To begin figuring out what you are passionate about, write down all the things you like to do when you are free or those you just have an innate interest in. Focus on things that interest you or that make you feel good.

Conversely, your values are the principles that you live by and use to inform your thoughts, feelings, and actions. They have an effect on your decision-making and the objectives you establish for yourself. Common values may include integrity, creativity, independence, helping others, or financial stability. Consider the things that have made you happy or sad; doing so can shed light on your fundamental principles.

Taking a personality test or other self-assessment tool is a great approach to learning more about your interests and values. These sites can help you identify your preferences, habits, and motives. Some common possibilities include the Holland Code, the Strong Interest Inventory, and the Values in Action Inventory. However, it's vital to approach these assessments with an open mind and realize that they are designed to be helpful tools, not definitive designations.

Another excellent practice is to conduct informational interviews with professionals on topics that interest you. Asking questions about their daily activities, problems, and sources of satisfaction might help you better understand if their employment corresponds with your interests and values.

As you develop clarity on your interests and values, explore how they overlap and influence your job objectives. For example, if you value creativity and have an interest in technology, a career in graphic design, web development, or user experience (UX) design would be a suitable fit.

Remember, your interests and values may shift throughout time, and that's entirely natural. Embrace this process as an opportunity for self-discovery and growth. By regularly connecting your employment choices with your real interests and values, you boost your chances of finding a happy and meaningful path.

Identifying Your Unique Strengths and Talents

Every individual has a unique blend of abilities and talents that can influence their career path. Identifying and exploiting these strengths is key to finding a rewarding and successful profession that corresponds with your abilities and passions.

Strengths are the inherent abilities and attributes that come readily to you and help you to flourish in particular areas. They can be cognitive, such as analytical thinking or problem-solving, or non-cognitive, like creativity, empathy, or leadership. Talents, on the other hand, are the abilities or aptitudes that you have developed through practice and experience.

To determine your abilities and talents, start by reflecting on the tasks or activities you find yourself succeeding at with relative ease. These could be academic disciplines, extracurricular activities, or personal pursuits. Pay attention to the areas where you frequently receive great feedback or produce remarkable results with minimal effort.

Another important practice is to obtain comments from individuals who know you well, such as family members, instructors, coaches, or mentors. Their outside perspective can frequently highlight traits and talents that you may ignore or take for granted.

Self-assessment tools like the VIA Character Skills Survey or the Gallup StrengthsFinder can also provide significant insights into your particular skills and talents. These evaluations are designed to determine your dominant qualities and abilities, which can inform your career exploration.

Once you have recognized your abilities and talents, explore how they might be applied to various career options. For example, if you thrive in communication and public speaking, employment in marketing, sales, or public relations may be a good fit. If you have great analytical and problem-solving abilities, you might thrive in professions like data analysis, engineering, or research.

It's vital to highlight that while your abilities and talents can lead to your job choices, they should not limit you. Many successful persons have found ways to nurture new abilities and strengthen their weaker areas via dedication and effort. However, starting from a foundation of your natural abilities and talents can provide a major edge and a sense of pleasure in your chosen vocation.

Remember, your strengths and talents are unique to you, and recognizing them can set you apart in the job market and contribute to your overall pleasure and success in your profession.

Finding Inspiration: Role Models and Success Stories

As you embark on your career planning path, surrounding yourself with inspiring role models and success stories can provide important motivation and guidance. These folks can serve as live examples of what is possible, offering insights and tactics that can help define your path.

Role models are individuals whose achievements, morals, or personal experiences resonate with you and motivate you to strive for greatness. They might come from many backgrounds and industries, and their influence can extend beyond their professional accomplishments.

Start by selecting role models within your immediate networks, such as family members, teachers, coaches, or community leaders. Observe the qualities and features that you respect in them, and consider how they have navigated their careers and surmounted hurdles.

Expand your search to public personalities, entrepreneurs, or prominent individuals in your areas of interest. Follow their adventures, read their biographies or autobiographies, and analyze their ways to success. Attending professional events, networking opportunities, or guest speaker sessions can also provide an opportunity to engage with possible role models in person.

Success tales, on the other hand, are real-life instances of persons who have achieved great feats or overcome tremendous difficulties to fulfill their goals. These stories can motivate you and demonstrate that success is feasible, regardless of your starting place or circumstances.

Seek out success stories from varied sources, such as books, periodicals, podcasts, or internet platforms. Pay attention to the techniques, mindsets, and resilience demonstrated by these individuals, and evaluate how you may apply similar ideas to your journey.

Additionally, look for success stories that relate to your unique history, interests, or obstacles. These relatable stories can provide significant insights and practical recommendations adapted to your circumstances.

As you examine role models and success stories, engage with them actively. Take notes, reflect on the lessons learned, and explore how you may adapt and apply these insights to your career planning process.

Remember, role models and success stories are not meant to be idealized or mindlessly imitated. Instead, use them as sources of inspiration and guidance, while keeping true to your actual self and unique circumstances.

By surrounding yourself with inspiring persons and stories, you may create a growth mindset, stay motivated, and obtain vital insights to help you navigate your career journey with confidence and perseverance.

Chapter Two

Navigating the Modern Career Landscape

Traditional vs. Non-Traditional Career Paths

In the past, career pathways were often more linear and predictable, with individuals pursuing a traditional route that comprised finishing formal schooling, finding a position in their area, and ascending through a hierarchical structure within an organization. However, the current career landscape has transformed, presenting a varied range of possibilities that defy the established conventions.

Traditional Career Paths:

Traditional career routes often involve pursuing a well-established profession or industry, requiring a specific degree or certification. These pathways are characterized by an organized progression, with clearly defined roles and duties within an organization. Examples of traditional professional routes include:

- Medicine (doctors, nurses, pharmacists)
- Law (lawyers, judges, legal professions)
- Education (teachers, professors, administrators)
- Engineering (civil, mechanical, electrical, etc.)
- Accounting and Finance (accountants, financial analysts, bankers)

While traditional career pathways offer a certain level of stability and security, they may also be regarded as more rigid and less adaptable to changing market conditions or personal preferences.

Non-Traditional Career Paths:

Non-traditional job pathways, on the other hand, are frequently more flexible, unconventional, and adapted to individual interests and objectives. These approaches may entail a combination of formal education, self-directed learning, and practical experience. They can span multiple industries or jobs, allowing for better career mobility and exploration. Examples of non-traditional job trajectories include:

- Freelancing and Gig Work (graphic design, writing, consulting, etc.)
- Entrepreneurship and Business Ownership
- Portfolio Careers (combining multiple part-time pursuits)
- Creative and Artistic Endeavors (music, movies, art, etc.)
- Remote Work and Digital Nomadism

Non-traditional professional choices give the ability to break free from conventional restraints, embrace freedom, and pursue hobbies or alternative lifestyles. However, they may also come with higher unpredictability, financial hazards, and the need for self-discipline and self-motivation.

As you examine your career alternatives, it's crucial to grasp the benefits and downsides of both traditional and non-traditional paths. Traditional paths may provide more structure and security, whereas non-traditional paths offer greater flexibility and autonomy. The goal is to fit your choice with your values, hobbies, and lifestyle preferences.

It's also worth mentioning that the distinctions between traditional and non-traditional professional routes are getting increasingly blurred. Many individuals are now embracing hybrid techniques, integrating components of both courses or switching between them during their careers. This fluidity reflects the dynamic nature of the modern employment environment and the significance of flexibility and lifelong learning.

Regardless of the path you take, it's crucial to be open-minded, interested, and willing to explore new opportunities as they occur. By remaining updated about current trends and changes, you may traverse the career landscape with confidence and make informed decisions that match your goals and desires.

Future-Proof Jobs and Emerging Trends

The world of labor is continually evolving, pushed by technology breakthroughs, globalization, and shifting socio-economic forces. As a result, certain vocations and industries are anticipated to have significant growth and demand in the next few years, while others may face disruption or collapse. Staying informed on future-proof employment and emerging trends can help you make strategic career choices and position yourself for long-term success.

Future-Proof Jobs:
Future-proof employment is less likely to be automated or made redundant by technology breakthroughs and is projected to remain in high demand in the foreseeable future. Some examples of future-proof jobs include:

1. Healthcare Professionals (nurses, physicians, medical technicians)
2. STEM Careers (science, technology, engineering, mathematics)
3. Data & Analytics Specialists (data scientists, business intelligence analysts)
4. Cybersecurity Experts (information security analysts, ethical hackers)
5. Skilled Trades (electricians, plumbers, HVAC technicians)
6. Creative and Design Roles (graphic designers, user experience designers)

7. Mental Health Professionals (psychologists, counselors, therapists)

8. Renewable Energy Technicians (solar panel installers, wind turbine technicians)

These positions frequently demand specialized skills, critical thinking, problem-solving abilities, and human interaction, which are less susceptible to automation or offshore.

Emerging Trends:

To future-proof occupations, it's crucial to remain ahead of emerging trends that are influencing the labor market and creating new opportunities. Some major trends to watch for include:

1. **Artificial Intelligence and Machine Learning**: As AI and machine learning technologies continue to evolve, new job responsibilities will emerge in areas such as AI development, data labeling, and algorithm monitoring.

2. Internet of Things (IoT) and Smart Technology: The proliferation of linked devices and smart systems will boost demand for individuals proficient in IoT development, cybersecurity, and data analysis.

3. Remote Work and Virtual Collaboration: The COVID-19 epidemic has hastened the transition towards remote work and virtual collaboration, offering opportunities for remote-friendly occupations and technologies that allow remote work.

4. Green and Sustainable Industries: With an increasing focus on environmental sustainability, jobs in renewable energy, sustainable agriculture, and eco-friendly product development are likely to grow.

5. E-Commerce and Digital Marketing: As more firms adopt digital platforms and online sales, roles in e-commerce, digital marketing, and social media management will continue to be in high demand.

6. tailored Services and Experiences: Industries that offer tailored services and experiences, such as premium hotels, concierge services, and customized product development, are positioned for growth.

By keeping an eye on these developing trends, you can position yourself to acquire the essential skills and information needed to capitalize on new opportunities as they occur.

It's crucial to recognize that while some careers may be more future-proof than others, no vocation is fully immune to change and upheaval. Developing a mindset of lifelong learning, adaptability, and continual skill improvement is vital for long-term career success in an ever-evolving employment environment.

Entrepreneurship and Side Hustles for Teens

Entrepreneurship and side hustles offer youngsters a unique opportunity to explore their hobbies, develop vital skills, and gain real-world experience while still in their formative years. These pastimes not only give financial benefits but also nurture vital skills like creativity, problem-solving, and resilience, which may be invaluable assets in any future job path.

Entrepreneurship:
Entrepreneurship involves the conception, development, and administration of a business enterprise. For youth, entrepreneurial pursuits can take several forms, such as:

1. **Product-based businesses:** Creating and selling actual things like apparel, accessories, or handcrafted crafts through internet platforms or local markets.

2. **Service-based businesses:** Offering services like tutoring, pet care, lawn care, or computer/tech help within the local community.

3. **Online businesses:** Leveraging the internet to offer digital products or services like graphic design, web development, virtual support, or content creation.

4. **Social entrepreneurship**: Developing a business model that tackles social or environmental challenges while generating cash.

Starting a business as a teen can be a useful learning experience, teaching critical skills like market research, financial management, marketing, and customer service. It also promotes skills like initiative, risk-taking, and tenacity, which are highly prized in the modern workforce.

Side Hustles:

Side hustles are part-time or freelance gigs that kids can pursue alongside their schooling or other responsibilities. These can be a terrific way to explore other interests, earn extra pay, and obtain significant experience. Some common side hustle ideas for teens include:

1. Freelancing: Offering services like writing, graphic design, programming, or social media management through online marketplaces like Fiverr or Upwork.

2. Reselling and flipping: Sourcing and reselling things for a profit, either online or at local flea markets or garage sales.

3. Tutoring or teaching: Providing academic tutoring or teaching talents like music, painting, or athletics to younger kids.

4. Content creation: Develop a following on platforms like YouTube, TikTok, or Instagram by creating and distributing entertaining content.

5. Virtual assistance: Providing administrative or clerical support to organizations or individuals on a distant basis.

Side hustles not only bring monetary rewards but also offer excellent opportunities to develop transferable skills, build a professional network, and explore potential career pathways.

When pursuing entrepreneurship or side hustles, it's crucial to perform thorough research, build a sound business plan, and seek help from mentors or experienced professionals. Additionally, kids should prioritize their studies and establish a healthy balance between their ventures and other commitments.

Embracing entrepreneurship and side hustles at an early age can create a mindset of self-reliance, ingenuity, and adaptability, which are vital assets in the dynamic and ever-changing modern employment landscape.

Chapter Three

Setting SMART Career Goals

Short-term and Long-term Goal Setting

Effective goal formulation is a critical component of successful career planning. By creating both short-term and long-term goals, you can develop a roadmap that leads your activities, measures your progress, and keeps you encouraged throughout your path. The key is to ensure that your goals are SMART: Specific, Measurable, Achievable, Relevant, and Time-bound.

Short-term Goals:
Short-term goals can be fulfilled within a relatively short time frame, often ranging from a few weeks to

a year or two. These goals serve as stepping stones toward your long-term aspirations and help you retain focus and momentum. Examples of short-term career aspirations for youths can include:

1. Maintaining a specified grade point average (GPA) or academic performance level.
2. Completing a meaningful internship or acquiring real work experience in a field of interest.
3. Developing a certain talent or ability, such as coding, graphic design, or public speaking.
4. Participating in extracurricular activities or leadership roles that coincide with your job interests.
5. Networking and creating connections with professionals in your target sector or subject.

Short-term goals should be specific, measurable, and feasible within the provided time frame. They should also be relevant to your long-term job objectives and linked with your beliefs and priorities.

Long-term Goals:

Long-term goals are the overarching objectives that steer your career journey over a longer extended period, generally lasting several years or even decades. These goals define your ultimate vision and provide a sense of direction and purpose. Examples of long-term career ambitions for youths can include:

1. Obtaining a specific degree or professional certification in your chosen sector.
2. Securing a desired job or position inside a certain industry or firm.
3. Starting your firm or becoming an entrepreneur in a given area.
4. Achieving a leadership or executive post within your chosen profession.
5. Making a substantial contribution or impact within your field or community.

Long-term goals should be ambitious yet feasible, and they should be associated with your values, hobbies, and personal qualities. It's necessary to break down these long-term goals into smaller, practical actions and milestones to ensure a clear path toward their accomplishment.

Regularly analyzing and updating your short-term and long-term goals is vital as your circumstances, priorities, and aspirations may change over time. Embrace flexibility and be open to altering your goals as needed, while retaining a strong commitment to your overarching vision and purpose.

By creating both short-term and long-term SMART objectives, you may create a systematic and meaningful approach to your career planning, stay motivated, and consistently work toward reaching your aspirations.

Creating a Personalized Career Roadmap

A tailored career roadmap is a thorough strategy that explains the stages and tactics you need to take to attain your long-term career goals. It acts as a roadmap that helps you negotiate the complicated and ever-changing terrain of the modern workforce while ensuring that your decisions and actions remain aligned with your unique interests, values, and talents.

Developing a personalized career plan requires several critical components:

1. **Self-assessment:** Begin by doing a thorough self-assessment to discover your interests, values, abilities, and strengths. This stage will help you identify your natural inclinations and talents, which will shape your job options.

2. Goal setting: Establish both short-term and long-term SMART goals that match your self-assessment and aspirations. These goals will serve as the cornerstone for your professional plan, offering direction and measurable milestones along the way.

3. study and exploration: Conduct an extensive study on potential career routes, industries, and work opportunities that align with your goals and interests. Explore educational requirements, job prospects, growth opportunities, and potential hurdles within each sector.

4. Skill development plan: Identify the skills and competencies required for your preferred career path and build a strategy to acquire or increase those talents. This may involve formal schooling, training programs, certificates, internships, or self-directed learning opportunities.

5. Network building: Actively seek out and create relationships with professionals, mentors, and industry experts within your sector of interest. These contacts can provide crucial information, recommendations, and future career or internship possibilities.

6. Experiential learning: Incorporate practical experiences into your path, such as internships, part-time jobs, volunteering, or business projects. These hands-on opportunities will help you to use your abilities, receive real-world exposure, and better understand the reality of your chosen career path.

7. Flexible adaptation: Recognize that your career roadmap is not set in stone. Be prepared to modify and adjust your plan when you gain new insights, meet unforeseen problems, or as your hobbies and goals evolve.

8. Timeline and milestones: Establish realistic deadlines and milestones for reaching your goals, taking into account aspects such as educational needs, financial concerns, and personal situations.

Your career roadmap should be a dynamic document that you frequently examine and change as appropriate. It should act as a guide but also allow for flexibility and adaptation as you negotiate the ever-changing world of work.

By building a detailed and individualized career roadmap, you may approach your career journey with intention, focus, and a clear awareness of the tasks required to reach your ambitions.

Overcoming Obstacles and Staying Motivated

Pursuing a meaningful and happy job path is a journey filled with challenges and barriers. From self-doubt and procrastination to external setbacks and competitiveness, there will be moments when your motivation and determination will be tested. Developing solutions to overcome these challenges and maintain a high level of motivation is vital for long-term success.

Identifying and Addressing Obstacles:
The first step in conquering barriers is to understand and acknowledge the various roadblocks that may develop along your career journey. Common hurdles faced by teens and young professionals include:

1. Lack of experience or qualifications
2. Financial restraints or restricted resources
3. Negative self-talk or impostor syndrome
4. Peer pressure or societal expectations
5. Balancing multiple priorities (school, work, extracurriculars)
6. Rejection or failure in employment applications or interviews
7. Uncertainty about career objectives or direction

Once you've recognized the potential hurdles, it's necessary to establish a plan to address them proactively. This may involve obtaining help from mentors or professional counselors, earning more skills or training, altering your timeframe or goals, or investigating alternate options.

Building a Support System:
Having a solid support system can be important in conquering problems and staying motivated. Surround yourself with individuals who believe in your potential and promote your objectives. This

could be family members, friends, instructors, counselors, or specialists in your intended sector.

Seek mentors or role models who have traversed similar issues and can provide significant insights and assistance. Joining professional organizations, networking groups, or online communities relating to your job interests can help connect you with like-minded others who can offer support and encouragement.

Cultivating a Positive Mindset:
Your thinking plays a significant part in conquering problems and retaining motivation. Adopting a growth mindset, which accepts problems as opportunities for learning and growth, can help you reframe setbacks and failures as meaningful experiences rather than permanent roadblocks.

Practice positive self-talk and fight negative thoughts or self-doubt. Celebrate minor triumphs and accomplishments along the way, since these can offer a sense of progress and momentum.

Engaging in activities that promote mental and physical well-being, such as exercise, mindfulness practices, or hobbies, can also help you manage stress and maintain a good outlook.

Setting Realistic Goals and Timelines:
Unrealistic expectations or too-ambitious ambitions can lead to frustration and demotivation. It's crucial to develop reasonable and measurable goals that match your present abilities and resources. Break down large goals into smaller, incremental actions to produce a sense of accomplishment and progress.

Be flexible and willing to change your goals and timetables as needed. Unexpected events or new possibilities may develop, and it's crucial to alter your plans accordingly while keeping your overarching vision in mind.

Seeking Professional Support:

In some circumstances, getting professional guidance may be important to overcome specific difficulties or address underlying issues that are influencing your motivation and career progress. Career counselors, life coaches, or mental health specialists can provide tailored assistance, methods, and resources to help you manage problems and restore a sense of direction and purpose.

Remember, problems and disappointments are inevitable on every career path. However, by developing resilience, cultivating a strong support system, and having a positive and adaptive mentality, you may overcome these hurdles and stay motivated in pursuit of your ambitions.

Chapter Four

Developing Essential Skills for Success

Communication and Interpersonal Skills

Effective communication and good interpersonal skills are necessary for success in every career path. These talents not only enable you to explain your ideas and thoughts clearly but also help you develop meaningful connections, cooperate effectively, and handle numerous professional and personal circumstances with confidence.

Verbal Communication:

Verbal communication covers your capacity to communicate yourself clearly and convincingly through spoken words. Developing good verbal communication abilities involves:

1. Active listening: Practicing active listening means giving your entire attention, making eye contact, and avoiding interruptions when others are speaking.

2. Clarity and articulation: Speak slowly, and clearly, and use proper volume and tone to ensure your message is easily understood.

3. Body language: Being conscious of your body language, such as posture, gestures, and facial expressions, as they can strengthen or contradict your vocal message.

4. Public speaking: Practicing public speaking abilities through classroom presentations, joining a debating club, or participating in community events helps build confidence and composure while addressing groups.

Written Communication:

In today's digital world, written communication skills are crucial. Mastering written communication involves:

1. Proper grammar and spelling: Understanding and using the principles of grammar, punctuation, and spelling to convey your point effectively in writing.

2. Tone and style: Adapt your writing style and tone to suit the purpose and audience, whether it's a formal report, a casual email, or a social media post.

3. Proofreading and editing: Develop the habit of thoroughly proofreading and editing your written work to ensure accuracy, clarity, and professionalism.

4. Digital literacy: Being adept in using various digital communication tools, such as email, instant messaging, and collaborative platforms.

Interpersonal Skills:

Interpersonal skills are the qualities that enable you to communicate effectively with others, develop relationships, and work together. Key interpersonal abilities include:

1. Empathy and emotional intelligence: Understanding and responding correctly to the feelings and viewpoints of others, establishing trust and rapport.

2. Conflict resolution: Developing skills for resolving conflicts and handling differences productively and politely.

3. Teamwork and collaboration: Contributing productively to team efforts, valuing varied perspectives, and working towards common goals.

4. Networking and connection building: Initiating and maintaining professional ties, networking effectively, and developing a solid support system.

Continuously developing and polishing your communication and interpersonal skills is vital for personal and professional progress. Seek opportunities to practice these skills, such as participating in group projects, joining clubs or organizations, or attending courses or seminars focusing on communication and interpersonal development.

Remember, excellent communication and strong interpersonal skills are vital tools that will serve you well in any job path you pick and in all aspects of your life.

Critical Thinking and Problem-Solving

In today's quickly expanding employment market, the ability to think critically and solve problems efficiently is highly valued by employers across all industries. These talents enable you to analyze difficult situations, identify potential solutions, and make informed judgments, making you a great asset in any workplace.

Critical Thinking:
Critical thinking involves the ability to assess information objectively, identify patterns and connections, and develop logical conclusions. Developing excellent critical thinking skills involves:

1. **testing assumptions:** Challenging preconceived beliefs and testing the validity of assumptions to get a deeper understanding of a situation or problem.
2. **Evaluating evidence:** Assessing the credibility and significance of information from multiple sources to make educated decisions.
3. **Recognizing biases:** Identifying and minimizing personal biases, as well as biases present in information sources, to avoid inaccurate conclusions.

4. Considering numerous perspectives: Exploring diverse opinions and ways to acquire a more comprehensive knowledge of a topic or problem.

Problem-Solving:

Problem-solving abilities are directly connected to critical thinking and involve the capacity to identify and address issues or impediments methodically and effectively. Developing excellent problem-solving skills involves:

1. Problem identification: Clearly defining and understanding the fundamental cause of a problem or difficulty before attempting to fix it.

2. Brainstorming and ideation: Generating a range of prospective solutions or methods through creative thinking and investigation of numerous alternatives.

3. Analysis and evaluation: Carefully examining and assessing the prospective solutions, including their feasibility, dangers, and potential consequences.

4. Implementation and monitoring: Executing the chosen solution, monitoring its progress, and making adjustments as needed to ensure successful resolution of the problem.

Practical Strategies:

To build and strengthen your critical thinking and problem-solving skills, explore the following strategies:

1. Engage in activities that challenge your thinking: Participate in discussions, logic puzzles, case studies, or thought experiments that require you to examine material, spot patterns, and develop conclusions.

2. Practice active learning: Instead of passively consuming information, actively question, analyze, and apply what you learn to real-world circumstances.

3. Seek multiple perspectives: Expose yourself to new thoughts and ideas by reading widely, attending lectures or conversations, and engaging with individuals from diverse backgrounds.

4. Learn from setbacks and mistakes: Reflect on circumstances where your thinking or problem-solving technique fell short, and utilize those experiences as chances to learn and better.

5. Collaborate with others: Work in teams or groups, since varied viewpoints and teamwork can increase critical thinking and problem-solving abilities.

By developing strong critical thinking and problem-solving skills, you will be better ready to negotiate complicated circumstances, make informed judgments, and contribute meaningful solutions in whichever job path you choose.

Time Management and Productivity Hacks

In today's fast-paced environment, efficient time management and productivity tactics are vital for reaching your goals and maintaining a healthy work-life balance. With various demands and distractions clamoring for your attention, it's vital to build habits and strategies that help you stay focused, organized, and efficient.

Time Management Strategies:
Time management entails planning, prioritizing, and managing your time effectively to ensure that critical tasks and responsibilities are performed within targeted timeframes. Here are some excellent time management strategies:

1. Goal setting: Establish clear and defined goals, both short-term and long-term, to provide direction and emphasis for your work.

2. Prioritization: Identify and prioritize your tasks based on importance and urgency, utilizing strategies like the Eisenhower Matrix or the ABCDE method.

3. Time blocking: Dedicate discrete blocks of time for certain work or projects, minimizing distractions and enhancing attention.

4. Scheduling: Use a calendar or planner to schedule tasks, appointments, and deadlines, ensuring you provide ample time for each activity.

5. Batching: Group comparable jobs together and do them in batches, minimizing the time and mental effort required to transition between different types of tasks.

Productivity Hacks:

Productivity hacks are tactics and practices aimed to help you work more efficiently and optimize your production. Here are some powerful efficiency hacks:

1. Eliminate distractions: Identify and limit sources of distraction, such as social media messages, email alerts, or needless background noise, to maintain focus and concentration.

2. Pomodoro Technique: Use the Pomodoro Technique, which entails working in focused 25-minute intervals interspersed by brief breaks, to enhance concentration and reduce burnout.

3. Single-tasking: Resist the temptation of multitasking and instead focus on one activity at a time, as multitasking can lead to decreased productivity and greater errors.

4. Automate and streamline: Leverage technology and automation technologies to streamline repetitive procedures and eliminate manual effort, freeing up time for more vital pursuits.

5. Take pauses: Incorporate frequent breaks into your routine to recharge and sustain energy levels, as continuous labor without rest can lead to lower productivity and burnout.

Developing Personal Habits:

In addition to specific methods and hacks, building personal habits that help productivity and time management is vital. These habits may include:

1. Waking up early: Starting your day early can provide a devoted period of focused work before extraneous distractions and demands kick in.

2. Exercise and good habits: Maintaining a healthy lifestyle through exercise, proper nutrition, and adequate sleep will boost your energy levels, focus, and overall productivity.

3. Minimizing procrastination: Identify and address the core causes of procrastination, such as fear of failure or lack of enthusiasm, to overcome this productivity-hindering behavior.

4. Continuous learning: Regularly seek out opportunities to learn new time management and productivity skills, and change your approach as needed to suit your changing circumstances and goals.

Remember, good time management and productivity tactics are extremely personal, and may take a trial to find the approach that works best for you. Be patient, stay committed, and continually endeavor to optimize your use of time and energy for optimal productivity and personal growth.

Chapter Five

Gaining Real-World Experience

Internships and Apprenticeships 101

Internships and apprenticeships are important opportunities for youth to obtain practical, hands-on experience in their subjects of interest, develop essential skills, and explore potential career options before committing to a specific path. These experiences not only enrich your resume and increase your competitiveness in the job market but also provide useful insights into other businesses and work situations.

Internships:

An internship is a temporary, supervised work experience that allows you to get practical exposure to a particular sector or career. Internships can be paid or unpaid, and they normally continue for a specified term, ranging from a few weeks to many months.

Benefits of internships:
1. **Practical application of knowledge:** Internships provide an opportunity to apply the theoretical knowledge obtained in the classroom to real-world settings, reinforcing your learning and expanding your understanding of the topic.
2. **Skill development:** You can build and polish critical abilities such as problem-solving, communication, teamwork, and time management, which are highly desired by employers.
3. **Professional networking:** Internships allow you to create professional relationships and connections within your target field, which might lead to potential career possibilities or valuable recommendations in the future.

4. Career exploration: By experiencing numerous positions and responsibilities within a company, you can better assess if a particular career path corresponds with your interests, strengths, and aspirations.

Finding and getting internships:

1. Start your search early: Many companies and organizations have specified application schedules for internships, so start your search well in advance.

2. Utilize your school's career center: Your high school or college career center can give valuable resources, like internship listings, resume assistance, and networking opportunities.

3. Leverage your network: Reach out to family, friends, teachers, or people in your intended field to inquire about prospective internship possibilities or build connections.

4. Tailor your application: Customize your CV, cover letter, and application materials to highlight your relevant abilities, experiences, and interest in the specific internship opportunity.

5. **Prepare for interviews:** Practice your interviewing skills, research the company or organization, and be prepared to articulate why you are a viable candidate for the internship.

Apprenticeships:

An apprenticeship is a structured training program that combines on-the-job training with classroom education. Apprenticeships are often longer-term commitments, lasting ranging from one to six years, and are often focused on specialized trades or technical vocations.

Benefits of apprenticeships:

1. **Hands-on training:** Apprenticeships give substantial hands-on training under the leadership of experienced professionals, allowing you to develop practical skills and knowledge directly applicable to your chosen industry.

2. **make while you learn:** Most apprenticeships offer paid work, allowing you to make a salary while

obtaining useful experience and avoiding considerable college debt.

3. Industry-recognized credentials: Upon successful completion of an apprenticeship program, you obtain industry-recognized credentials or certifications, enhancing your employability and earning potential.

4. Mentorship and networking: Apprenticeships generally involve close mentorship from experienced professionals, giving essential guidance and networking possibilities within the field.

Finding and securing apprenticeships:

1. Research industry-specific programs: Many industries, such as construction, manufacturing, and skilled trades, provide apprenticeship programs through unions, trade groups, or individual companies.

2. Check with your school's career center: Some high schools and colleges have agreements with local firms offering apprenticeship opportunities.

3. Explore government resources: Organizations like the Department of Labor or state-level workforce development agencies can provide information on available apprenticeship programs in your area.

4. Meet eligibility requirements: Apprenticeship programs may have strict eligibility requirements, such as age, education level, or prerequisites, so check you meet these criteria before applying.

5. Prepare for interviews and assessments: Apprenticeship interviews and assessments may include written examinations, practical demonstrations, or interviews to evaluate your skills and fit for the program.

Whether you take an internship or an apprenticeship, these real-world experiences are crucial for personal and professional growth. They provide a competitive edge, practical skills, and a greater awareness of various career choices, putting you up for success as you navigate the workforce.

Volunteering and Community Involvement

Volunteering and community involvement are effective methods to obtain valuable real-world experience, develop essential skills, and have a positive influence on your local community or cause you care about. These experiences not only promote your personal and professional growth but also exhibit your devotion, initiative, and values to potential employers or educational institutions.

Benefits of Volunteering:

1. Skill development: Volunteering helps you to build and practice a wide range of transferable skills, such as communication, teamwork, problem-solving, time management, and leadership, which are highly valued in any career path.

2. **Networking and contacts:** Through volunteering, you can meet and interact with individuals from varied backgrounds, build your professional network, and potentially get insights or connections that could lead to future possibilities.

3. **Personal growth and fulfillment:** Engaging in volunteer work can enhance your confidence, widen your perspectives, and provide a feeling of purpose and fulfillment by making a positive impact on individuals or issues you care about.

4. **CV enhancement:** Volunteering indicates initiative, commitment, and a well-rounded character, which can make your CV stand out and create discussion points during the job or college interviews.

Finding Volunteer Opportunities:
1. **Check with local organizations:** Many non-profit organizations, community centers,

houses of worship, and schools have continuing volunteer opportunities and activities.

2. Explore online platforms: Websites like VolunteerMatch, Idealist, and local government portals can help you identify volunteer opportunities based on your interests, talents, and geography.

3. Participate in community activities or drives: Look for chances to volunteer at local events, fundraisers, or community service projects, such as food drives, park clean-ups, or charity runs.

4. Leverage your interests and passions: Seek volunteer opportunities linked to your hobbies, interests, or causes you care about since this will make the experience more meaningful and pleasurable.

Community Involvement:
Beyond typical volunteering, engaging in community involvement activities can also provide essential real-world experience and help your

personal and professional growth. Examples of community involvement include:

1. Joining student organizations or clubs: Participating in school-based clubs or organizations linked to your hobbies or career objectives can help you build leadership abilities, networking opportunities, and hands-on experience.

2. Attending community meetings or forums: Attending local government meetings, town halls, or community forums can expose you to critical topics and decision-making processes within your community.

3. Participating in youth councils or advisory boards: Many communities have youth councils or advisory boards that provide opportunities for young people to voice their ideas, engage in decision-making processes, and contribute to local initiatives.

4. Organizing or engaging in community service projects: Initiating or participating in community service projects, such as neighborhood clean-ups, fundraisers, or awareness campaigns, can display your leadership, organizational, and project management skills.

When engaging in volunteering or community participation activities, it's crucial to approach these encounters with professionalism, devotion, and a readiness to learn. Actively seek out opportunities to take on responsibility, collaborate with people, and share your talents and thoughts. Additionally, be careful to chronicle your experiences, successes, and the skills you've developed, since these can be excellent assets for your résumé, college applications, or future job interviews.

Starting a Business or Side Gig

In today's dynamic and entrepreneurial-driven economy, starting a business or pursuing side employment can be a vital chance for kids to obtain real-world experience, develop essential skills, and explore their interests and passions. Whether it's a small-scale initiative or a more ambitious entrepreneurial endeavor, these experiences can provide a unique learning path and potentially establish the groundwork for future job success.

Starting a Business:
Launching your own business may be a tough yet rewarding venture. Here are some steps to take while starting a business as a teen:

1. Identify your company idea: Explore your hobbies, talents, and passions to generate a business idea that corresponds with your capabilities and market demand. Conduct market research to analyze the viability and prospective competition for your product or service.

2. Develop a business plan: Create a detailed business plan that describes your goals, target market, product or service offers, marketing strategy, financial predictions, and operational information. This strategy will serve as a roadmap for your firm and can also help get funding or support if needed.

3. Secure finance: Determine the first cash requirements for your firm and seek funding possibilities such as personal savings, family support, crowdfunding platforms, or small business loans or grants specifically tailored for young entrepreneurs.

4. Establish legal and operational structures: Research the legal requirements for beginning a business in your location, such as registering your business name, acquiring relevant licenses or permissions, and comprehending tax duties. Additionally, establish operational procedures and processes to ensure effective and professional service delivery.

5. Market and promote your business: Develop a marketing strategy to promote your firm and reach your target audience. This may entail building an online presence (website, social media), networking, advertising, or utilizing local resources and events.

6. Continuously learn and adapt: Entrepreneurship is a continuous learning adventure. Be receptive to comments, adjust to changing market conditions, and seek mentorship or help from experienced entrepreneurs or business professionals.

Pursuing a Side Gig:
A side gig, also known as a side hustle or a freelance gig, is a part-time job or project that you take on in addition to your principal commitments, such as education or a full-time career. Side gigs can provide valuable real-world experience, additional pay, and the ability to explore alternative interests

or career choices. Some examples of side employment for teens include:

1. Freelance work: Offering services such as writing, graphic design, web development, tutoring, or content production on a freelance basis through internet platforms or local networking.

2. Reselling or flipping items: Sourcing and reselling stuff for a profit, either online (e.g., through e-commerce platforms) or at local markets or events.

3. Creative pursuits: Monetizing creative talents such as photography, videography, art, music, or handicraft by offering services or selling items.

4. Virtual assistance: Providing administrative, social media management, or customer service support remotely for organizations or people.

5. Peer-to-peer services: Offering services such as ride-sharing, task-running, or local delivery using peer-to-peer platforms.

When pursuing a side gig, it's crucial to manage your time properly, maintain a professional approach, and produce high-quality work or services. Building a great reputation and excellent ratings can lead to more possibilities and potential long-term success.

Starting a business or pursuing a side project can provide invaluable real-world experience, helping you to build entrepreneurial skills, problem-solving ability, and a greater understanding of the practical aspects of running an enterprise. These experiences can also help you explore potential career choices, create a professional network, and potentially produce income while still in your teens.

Chapter Six

Acing Academics and Extracurriculars

Balancing School, Activities, and Career Prep

As a teenager, striking the perfect balance between academics, extracurricular activities, and job preparation can be a tough endeavor. However, mastering this balance is vital for your personal growth, academic performance, and future professional opportunities. By creating effective time management skills and prioritizing your responsibilities, you can excel in all areas while minimizing stress and burnout.

Time Management Strategies:

1. Create a timetable: Develop a thorough schedule that incorporates your classes, study time, extracurricular activities, and career preparation assignments. Use a planner, calendar software, or digital tool to arrange your agenda and ensure you devote ample time to each commitment.

2. Prioritize and plan: Identify your priorities and invest time accordingly. Plan for forthcoming projects, assignments, and deadlines to reduce last-minute stress and ensure you have enough time to finish work properly.

3. Batch similar jobs: Group similar tasks together, such as completing homework assignments for various classes or working on college applications. This method can help you keep concentration and enhance productivity.

4. Eliminate distractions: Identify and reduce potential distractions, such as social media, unneeded online browsing, or background noise, to improve your attention and productivity during designated study or work periods.

5. routine breaks and downtime: While it's necessary to be productive, it's as crucial to incorporate breaks and downtime into your routine. Regular breaks can help you refuel, retain focus, and prevent burnout.

Balancing Academics:

Academics should be a key priority during your high school years since your academic achievement can considerably affect your future educational and employment options.

1. Attend all classes and participate actively: Regular attendance and active involvement in class can help you stay interested, grasp the material better, and create strong relationships with teachers.

2. Seek academic support: Don't hesitate to seek aid when needed. Utilize resources like tutoring services, study groups, or office hours with teachers to clarify ideas and reinforce your understanding.

3. Develop successful study habits: Experiment with different study approaches, such as note-taking, flashcards, or practice quizzes, to find ways that work best for your learning style.

Extracurricular Involvement:
Extracurricular activities can give excellent possibilities for personal growth, skill development, and exploration of interests beyond academics.

1. Choose activities strategically: Select extracurricular activities that correspond with your interests, values, and prospective professional aspirations. Avoid overcommitting to too many activities, as quality participation is more significant than quantity.

2. Seek leadership responsibilities: Look for opportunities to take on leadership roles within clubs or organizations, since these experiences can help you build critical skills like teamwork, communication, and project management.

3. Maintain a balanced schedule: While extracurricular activities are crucial, ensure they don't absorb too much time and energy, leaving little opportunity for academics or career preparation.

Career Preparation:
Dedicating time to career inquiry and preparation can provide a useful head start as you navigate your future school and professional routes.

1. Explore career options: Attend career fairs, participate in job shadowing opportunities, or do informative interviews to acquire insights into numerous professions and industries.

2. improve relevant skills: Identify the skills and competencies required for your preferred professional path and explore opportunities to improve or refine them through coursework, projects, internships, or self-study.

3. Build a professional network: Attend industry events, join professional associations, or engage with professionals in your desired field to extend your network and obtain useful insights and advice.

Remember, obtaining a balanced and enjoyable high school experience needs conscious preparation, discipline, and a willingness to prioritize and make compromises when required. Seek help from family, instructors, or counselors when needed, and frequently reassess your priorities to ensure you maintain a healthy and productive balance.

Choosing the Right Educational Path

Choosing the correct educational path is a key decision that can drastically affect your future employment chances and your life journey. With several alternatives accessible, ranging from traditional four-year colleges and universities to vocational programs, trade schools, and online learning platforms, it's vital to thoroughly analyze your interests, ambitions, and personal circumstances to make an informed choice.

Factors to Consider:

1. Career goals: Reflect on your intended career path and examine the educational requirements and certifications needed for that field. Some jobs may demand a specific degree or certification, while others may offer several options.

2. Learning style and preferences: Assess your preferred learning style and educational environment. Do you thrive in a traditional classroom setting, or would you benefit from more hands-on, experiential learning opportunities? Consider aspects such as class sizes, teaching styles, and campus atmosphere.

3. Financial considerations: Evaluate the costs associated with alternative educational options, including tuition, fees, housing and board, and potential financial aid or scholarship opportunities. Develop a reasonable budget and plan for paying for your education.

4. Location and lifestyle: Consider the geographic location of the educational institution and its impact on your living conditions and general lifestyle. Factors such as proximity to home, college culture, and housing alternatives might influence your overall experience.

5. Extracurricular opportunities: Explore the extracurricular activities, clubs, organizations, and support services offered by possible schools. These can boost your personal growth, skill development, and networking chances.

Traditional Four-Year Colleges and Universities:

This path offers a wide choice of degree programs, from liberal arts to specialist fields, and gives a well-rounded educational experience. Attending a four-year college or university can open doors to many employment choices and often leads to increased earning potential over time.

Community Colleges and Associate's Degrees:

Community colleges provide affordable two-year associate's degree programs, vocational training, and the option to transfer credits to a four-year institution later. This course can be an ideal choice for people seeking a more cost-effective education or interested in specific career training programs.

Vocational and Trade Schools:
These institutions specialize in hands-on, skill-based instruction in sectors such as construction, automotive repair, healthcare, or culinary arts. Vocational and trade schools can give a direct gateway to employment in specialized crafts and sometimes involve apprenticeships or on-the-job training components.

Online and Distance Learning:
With the rise of online educational platforms, distance learning has become a flexible and accessible alternative for many students. Online programs can offer a varied selection of degree programs, certifications, and self-paced learning possibilities, allowing you to match your studies with other responsibilities.

Gap Years and Alternative Paths:

Some students may choose to take a gap year before pursuing further education, using that time to get work experience, travel, or pursue personal interests. Others may opt for different options, such as entrepreneurship, military service, or straight entry into the workforce.

Regardless of the path you select, it's crucial to undertake thorough study, seek help from counselors or mentors, and thoroughly analyze the benefits and drawbacks of each option. Remember, your educational journey is not etched in stone, and you can always modify your course as your interests and ambitions evolve.

Navigating College Applications and Finances

The college application process might be frightening, but with good planning and preparation, you can navigate it effectively. From researching and selecting possible colleges to completing applications and receiving financial aid, each process demands careful study and attention to detail.

Researching and Selecting Colleges:
1. Identify your priorities: Determine the things that are most important to you, such as location, size, academic programs, campus life, and cost.

2. Utilize college search tools: Explore internet resources like college search engines, virtual tours, and college fairs to investigate and compare potential institutions.

3. Develop a balanced list: Create a list of reach, target, and safety schools depending on your academic profile and the admission standards of each university.

4. Visit campuses: When possible, attend campus tours and information sessions to acquire a personal understanding of the college environment and culture.

Preparing Your Applications:

1. Start early: Begin the application process well in advance to ensure you have adequate time to finish all required components, such as essays, letters of recommendation, and extra materials.

2. Craft interesting essays: Your college essays are an opportunity to demonstrate your unique personality, experiences, and objectives. Dedicate time and effort to writing well-written and intelligent essays that stand out.

3. Request letters of recommendation: Identify instructors, counselors, or mentors who can give good letters of recommendation showcasing your academic abilities and personal traits.

4. examine and revise: Carefully examine and proofread your applications to guarantee accuracy and completeness before submitting.

Securing Financial Aid:
Financing a college education can be a huge financial burden, but there are different options and tactics available to assist reduce the costs.

1. Complete the FAFSA: The Free Application for Federal Student Aid (FAFSA) is the gateway to accessing federal, state, and institutional financial aid. Complete the FAFSA as early as possible to optimize your aid eligibility.

2. Explore scholarship opportunities: Actively seek for and apply to scholarships granted by institutions, organizations, or private entities based on academic merit, extracurricular achievements, or personal circumstances.

3. Consider work-study programs: Many institutions provide work-study programs that allow students to earn revenue through part-time employment on campus, contributing to their educational expenses.

4. Investigate student loans: If necessary, investigate and comprehend the numerous forms of student loans, including federal and private loans, and their respective interest rates, repayment terms, and eligibility criteria.

5. Seek financial literacy resources: Develop a good understanding of personal finance and budgeting skills to properly manage your education spending and prevent excessive debt.

Navigating the college application and financial aid process can be tough, but with appropriate planning, organization, and perseverance, you can boost your chances of receiving admission to your selected colleges and securing the necessary financial resources.

Remember to seek help from school counselors, visit college fairs and information sessions, and harness online tools to keep informed and on track throughout the process.

Chapter Seven

Building Your Personal Brand

Creating an Online Portfolio and Presence

In today's digital world, creating a strong online presence and portfolio is vital for showing your skills, achievements, and personal brand. Whether you're pursuing jobs, internships, or educational possibilities, an attractive online portfolio may set you apart from the competition and provide a thorough picture of your capabilities.

Developing an Online Portfolio:

1. Choose a suitable platform: Decide on the ideal platform for your online portfolio, such as a personal website, a blog, or a portfolio hosting

provider like Wix, Squarespace, or WordPress. Consider things like customizing possibilities, ease of use, and mobile responsiveness.

2. Curate your best work: Carefully choose and organize your best projects, samples, or achievements that highlight your talents and knowledge. Include a varied selection of assets, such as written pieces, designs, coding projects, multimedia presentations, or visual artwork.

3. Craft appealing descriptions: Provide clear and concise explanations for each piece in your portfolio, detailing the context, aims, and issues you tackled. Highlight the skills and approaches you applied and any significant results or successes.

4. Showcase your uniqueness: While retaining professionalism, inject your online portfolio with aspects that represent your unique personality, inventiveness, and personal brand. This can contain a personalized design, a well-written bio, or multimedia components like movies or podcasts.

5. Optimize for search engines: Ensure your online portfolio is search engine optimized (SEO) by integrating relevant keywords, meta descriptions, and alt tags for photos. This will boost the visibility and discoverability of your portfolio on search engines.

Building an Online Presence:
In addition to an online portfolio, creating a strong online presence across numerous platforms can help you interact with possible employers, industry leaders, and like-minded individuals.

1. Create professional social media profiles: Maintain active and professional profiles on appropriate social media platforms, such as LinkedIn, Twitter, or industry-specific networks. Share updates, join in debates, and demonstrate your knowledge and accomplishments.

2. Start a blog or personal website: Consider starting a blog or personal website to share your thoughts, insights, and experiences relating to your areas of interest or expertise. This might position you as a thought leader and demonstrate your passion and knowledge.

3. Engage with online communities: Participate in online forums, discussion groups, or industry-specific communities relating to your subject of interest. Contribute useful thoughts, ask questions, and network with professionals and peers.

4. Build an email list: Develop an email list to offer updates, newsletters, or relevant content to interested followers. This can help you retain contacts and promote yourself as a trusted source of information or insights.

5. **Monitor and manage your online reputation:** Regularly monitor your internet presence and reputation by conducting search engine inspections and setting up alerts for your name or related keywords. Address any negative or erroneous information swiftly and properly.

Remember, developing a good online portfolio and presence is an ongoing process that demands consistent effort and attention. Regularly update your portfolio with new projects or successes, communicate with your online networks, and continuously seek ways to exhibit your abilities and personal brand.

Networking and Making Connections

Networking and creating meaningful connections are crucial components of personal and professional progress. By developing a strong network, you can receive useful insights, locate mentors and supporters, and unearth prospective chances for internships, employment, or collaborations.

In-Person Networking:

1. Attend industry events and conferences: Participate in local or national events, conferences, or trade exhibitions about your subject of interest. These conferences allow opportunities to meet people, learn about industry trends, and maybe build key contacts.

2. Join professional associations or clubs: Become a member of professional associations, student organizations, or clubs compatible with your career ambitions. Attend meetings, workshops, or social events to network with like-minded folks and broaden your circle.

3. Seek out informational interviews: Reach out to professionals in your target field and request informational interviews. These informal conversations allow you to learn about their professional paths, gather insights, and maybe build contacts that could lead to future opportunities.

4. Attend career fairs and networking events: Participate in career fairs, job fairs, or networking events organized by your school, local groups, or companies. These events allow opportunity to engage with recruiters, employers, and industry leaders.

5. Leverage your existing connections: Don't underestimate the importance of your present network, including family members, friends, teachers, or mentors. Let them know about your job aims and goals, as they may be able to introduce you to valuable contacts or provide advice.

Online Networking:

In addition to in-person networking, employing online platforms and digital technologies can increase your reach and generate valuable contacts.

1. Optimize your social media presence: Maintain an active and professional presence on social media platforms like LinkedIn, Twitter, or industry-specific networks. Engage in debates, share useful articles, and network with professionals in your sector.

2. Join online communities and forums: Participate in online communities, forums, or discussion groups about your areas of interest. Contribute thoughts, ask questions, and communicate with other members to build relationships and promote yourself as a competent resource.

3. Attend virtual events and webinars: Explore virtual events, webinars, or online conferences that provide an opportunity to learn from industry professionals and network with others from across the world.

4. Collaborate on online projects: Seek out online collaborative projects, hackathons, or open-source initiatives that correspond with your interests and skills. Working alongside others can lead to excellent relationships and learning opportunities.

5. Leverage alumni networks: Connect with alumni from your high school, college, or institution through formal alumni networks or social media organizations. These contacts can bring useful insights, mentorship, or new career possibilities.

Effective networking is not only about collecting business cards or building surface-level connections. It's about developing true connections based on mutual respect, shared interests, and a willingness to support and grow from one another.

Approach networking with sincerity, actively listen and focus on bringing value to people in your contacts.

Remember, networking is a continuing process that demands consistent effort and follow-up. Nurture your connections by staying in touch, offering aid when possible, and expressing thanks for the support and guidance you receive along the road.

Developing Confidence and Self-Marketing Skills

Confidence and the ability to properly sell yourself are crucial assets in today's competitive job market and professional scene. By improving these abilities, you may present yourself compellingly and honestly, communicate your value, and boost your chances of success in many endeavors, whether it's getting a dream job, impressing potential clients, or exploring entrepreneurial enterprises.

Building Self-Confidence:
1. Identify and acknowledge your strengths: Take the time to reflect on your unique talents, skills, and successes. Recognize and accept your strengths, as this can increase your self-belief and confidence.

2. **Practice positive self-talk**: Counteract negative self-talk or limiting thoughts by intentionally replacing them with positive, empowering statements. Remind yourself of your capabilities and the progress you've achieved.

3. **Embrace failures and setbacks**: Understand that failures and setbacks are inevitable components of growth and personal development. Rather than viewing them as flaws, reframe them as opportunities for growth and resilience.

4. Seek out supportive mentors and role models: Surround yourself with individuals who believe in your potential and can provide direction, encouragement, and constructive feedback. Their support and belief in you might generate self-assurance.

5. Practice self-care: Taking care of your physical, mental, and emotional well-being can add greatly to your overall confidence. Prioritize activities that encourage self-care, such as exercise, mindfulness practices, or pursuing hobbies you enjoy.

Developing Self-Marketing Skills:
1. Craft a strong personal brand: Define your distinctive value proposition and the attributes that set you apart. Develop a personal brand that honestly reflects your abilities, values, and objectives.

2. Create a professional online presence: Build a strong online presence that highlights your abilities, achievements, and personal brand. This can include an online portfolio, professional social media profiles, and interesting digital content.

3. Master the art of storytelling: Learn to share your experiences, accomplishments, and aspirations in an engaging and relatable manner. Effective storytelling can help you connect with others and make a lasting impact.

4. Develop good communication skills: Hone your writing and vocal communication abilities, as these are vital for effectively marketing yourself during job interviews, networking events, or professional encounters.

5. Seek for public speaking opportunities: Step out of your comfort zone and embrace opportunities to present or speak in front of crowds. Public speaking abilities can raise your confidence and strengthen your ability to successfully explain your value proposition.

6. Leverage your network: Build and maintain a strong professional network that can help your self-marketing efforts. Seek out references, endorsements, or testimonials from reputable relationships that highlight your abilities and achievements.

Remember, gaining confidence and self-marketing skills is an ongoing process that involves consistent effort, self-reflection, and a willingness to venture out of your comfort zone. Embrace feedback and continuously work to refine and strengthen these vital skills.

By combining self-confidence with successful self-marketing methods, you can portray yourself compellingly and honestly, express your value effectively, and boost your chances of accomplishing your personal and professional goals.

Chapter Eight

Job Search and Interview Mastery

Crafting Winning Resumes and Cover Letters

Your resume and cover letter are frequently the first impressions a potential employer will have of you, making them vital components of a successful job search. Crafting engaging and personalized materials can dramatically boost your chances of receiving an interview and finally landing your chosen job.

Writing an Effective Resume:

1. Choose the proper format: The format of your resume should be chosen by your level of experience and the specific job you're looking for. Common forms include chronological (highlighting job experience in reverse chronological order), functional (emphasizing abilities and achievements), and combination (blending features of both).

2. Craft a dynamic summary or objective statement: At the beginning of your resume, include a simple yet engaging summary or objective statement that highlights your primary qualifications, strengths, and professional aspirations. This part should quickly attract the reader's attention and convey your fit for the role.

3. Highlight relevant experience and achievements: Detail your professional experience, internships, volunteer jobs, or extracurricular activities that are relevant to the job you're pursuing. Quantify your achievements and efforts whenever possible, using particular numbers, percentages, or measures to highlight your impact.

4. Showcase transferable skills: Even if you lack direct experience in a certain industry, stress the transferable skills you've learned, such as problem-solving, communication, teamwork, or leadership abilities. Employers prefer well-rounded people with various skill sets.

5. Tailor your content: Customize your resume for each job application by including keywords from the job description and emphasizing the qualifications and experiences that are most relevant to the specific role and firm.

6. Ensure a clean and orderly format: Use consistent formatting, clear section headings, and a simple, easy-to-read typeface. Pay attention to spacing, margins, and general visual appeal to create a clean and professional document.

Crafting a Compelling Cover Letter:

1. investigate the organization and role: Before drafting your cover letter, investigate the firm, its values, and the exact needs of the job you're applying for. This information will help you design your letter and highlight your fit for the post.

2. Engage the reader from the start: Begin your cover letter with a strong opening line that hooks the reader's interest and clearly states why you're the right candidate for the position.

3. Highlight your qualifications and achievements: Use the body of your cover letter to expound on your relevant qualifications, experiences, and achievements that correspond with the job requirements. Provide detailed examples that highlight your talents and accomplishments.

4. Express your passion and fit: Convey your real enthusiasm for the role and the firm, and explain how your beliefs, goals, and experiences coincide with the organization's mission and culture.

5. Close with a strong call to action: In your conclusion paragraph, confidently request an interview or opportunity to further discuss your qualifications. Thank the reader for their consideration and repeat your interest in the post.

6. Proofread and edit carefully: Ensure your cover letter is free from any spelling, grammatical, or punctuation problems. Have someone else check it for clarity and effectiveness before submitting it.

Remember, your resume and cover letter are potent marketing tools that can greatly improve your chances of landing an interview. Take the time to develop appealing and specialized materials that successfully highlight your qualifications, achievements, and suitability for the career you're pursuing.

Acing Job Interviews and Following Up

Interviews are a vital part of the job search process, and attending them needs rigorous preparation, good communication skills, and a solid understanding of how to present yourself in the best possible light. Additionally, following up after an interview can reflect your sustained interest and professionalism, thus setting you apart from other candidates.

Preparing for the Interview:

1. Research the firm and role: Gather as much information as possible about the company, its culture, products or services, and the precise role you're interviewing for. This knowledge will help you personalize your responses and ask smart questions during the interview.

2. Practice common interview questions: Prepare responses to popular interview questions, such as "Tell me about yourself," "What are your strengths and weaknesses?" and "Why are you interested in this role?" Practice your answers out loud to ensure clarity and confidence.

3. Prepare relevant examples and accomplishments: Be ready to present specific instances and accomplishments that demonstrate your relevant abilities and experiences. Quantify your successes whenever feasible to prove your influence.

4. Develop questions for the interviewer: Prepare insightful questions to ask the interviewer, exhibiting your enthusiasm and understanding about the organization and role. Avoid queries that can be easily addressed by researching the company's website.

5. Gather relevant documents and materials: Compile all the necessary documents, such as copies of your resume, portfolio, or work samples, and ensure they are organized and easily available during the interview.

Acing the Interview:

1. Make a positive first impression: Dress professionally, arrive early, and greet the interviewer with a firm handshake and a confident manner. Maintain good posture and eye contact throughout the interview.

2. Listen attentively and react thoughtfully: Pay close attention to the interviewer's questions, and take a moment to organize your thoughts before responding. Provide clear and succinct replies, and don't be hesitant to ask for clarification if needed.

3. Highlight your qualifications and fit: Throughout the interview, focus on demonstrating how your abilities, experiences, and personality correspond with the job criteria and corporate culture. Draw links between your background and the role you're interviewing for.

4. Ask intelligent questions: When given the opportunity, ask the questions you prepared, as well as any follow-up questions that come throughout the meeting. This displays your real interest and participation in the work and organization.

5. Express passion and gratitude: Convey your enthusiasm for the work and company during the interview. Thank the interviewer for their time and consideration, and indicate your desire to move forward with the process.

Following Up After the Interview:

1. Send a thank-you note: Within 24-48 hours after the interview, send a thoughtful thank-you note or email to the interviewer(s). Reiterate your interest in the role, highlight significant topics from the conversation, and show your appreciation for their time and consideration.

2. Follow up on any additional requests: If the interviewer requested extra information or materials from you, swiftly deliver what was asked for and thank them for the opportunity to provide further details.

3. Stay involved and patient: While waiting for a decision, continue investigating the company and role, and be prepared for potential follow-up interviews or further requests from the employer.

4. Evaluate and learn from the experience: If you're not picked for the post, respectfully accept the decision and seek feedback on areas for growth. Use this event as a learning opportunity to develop your interview abilities for future possibilities.

Remember, interviews are a two-way evaluation process – not only is the employer reviewing your fit for the post, but you're also evaluating if the company and position connect with your professional goals and beliefs. By thoroughly preparing, successfully communicating your qualifications, and professionally following up, you can boost your chances of acing the interview and establishing a lasting positive impression.

Exploring Alternative Job Search Strategies

While standard job search tactics, such as online job boards and submitting resumes, are commonly utilized, investigating alternative strategies might widen your prospects and boost your chances of getting your preferred role. In today's competitive job market, thinking outside the box and taking a proactive approach can set you apart from other candidates.

Networking and Making Connections:

1. Attend industry events and conferences: Participate in local or national events, conferences, or trade exhibitions about your subject of interest. These gatherings allow the opportunity to connect with people, learn about industry trends, and maybe unearth job openings or possibilities.

2. Leverage your existing network: Inform your family, friends, former colleagues, and mentors about your job search goals. They may be aware of possible opportunities or be able to introduce you to valuable connections within their networks.

3. Join professional associations or clubs: Become a member of professional associations, student organizations, or clubs compatible with your career ambitions. Attend meetings, workshops, or social events to broaden your network and maybe learn about employment openings or industry insights.

4. Use social media strategically: Leverage social media platforms like LinkedIn, Twitter, or industry-specific networks to connect with professionals in your preferred field, join relevant groups, and engage in discussions about job prospects or industry trends.

Informational Interviews and Job Shadowing:

1. **Conduct informational interviews**: Reach out to professionals in your target field and seek informational interviews. These informal conversations allow you to learn about their professional routes, receive insights into the sector, and maybe develop contacts that could lead to future opportunities.

2. **Pursue work shadowing opportunities**: Explore the possibilities of job shadowing professionals in professions or companies that interest you. This hands-on experience can provide vital insights into the day-to-day responsibilities, work environment, and culture of a particular career path.

Speculative Applications and Targeted Outreach:

1. **Submit speculative applications**: Even if a company doesn't have publicized job openings, try submitting a speculative application or resume to

convey your interest in working for the organization. This proactive attitude can often lead to unexpected possibilities or keep you top-of-mind for future openings.

2. Identify and target specific firms: Research companies or organizations that correspond with your professional goals and interests, then approach out directly to express your interest in potential employment openings or possibilities. This tailored strategy can be more effective than applying blindly to job advertisements.

Freelancing, Contracting, or Starting Your Own Business:

1. Explore freelance or contract work: Consider offering your talents and services as a freelancer or contractor in your desired field. This can help you obtain useful experience, establish a portfolio, and potentially lead to long-term work chances.

2. Start your own business or side hustle: If entrepreneurship coincides with your goals, try starting your own business or side hustle relevant to your hobbies and talents. This can exhibit your initiative, and entrepreneurial mindset, and provide significant real-world experience.

Remember, the job search process can be hard, but embracing a range of techniques and remaining proactive can boost your chances of success. Be open to exploring new options, continually networking, and showing your unique value to potential employers.

Chapter Nine

Embracing Diversity and Inclusion

Overcoming Challenges and Stereotypes

In today's varied culture, individuals from various backgrounds and identities often encounter unique problems and preconceptions that might impair their personal and professional success. However, by recognizing and eliminating these hurdles, you may foster a more inclusive and equitable atmosphere for yourself and others.

Understanding Stereotypes and Biases:
1. Identify stereotypes: Stereotypes are oversimplified generalizations about a certain group of individuals based on their race, ethnicity,

gender, religion, age, or other traits. It's necessary to recognize and acknowledge the presence of these prejudices to confront and demolish them successfully.

2. Examine unconscious biases: Unconscious biases are deeply ingrained attitudes or ideas that influence our behavior and decision-making processes without our conscious awareness. Becoming conscious of your personal biases is the first step towards resolving and limiting their impact.

3. Educate yourself: Seek out credible sources of knowledge, attend diversity and inclusion programs, or engage with persons from diverse backgrounds to learn about their experiences and viewpoints. Understanding other cultures, identities, and lived experiences can help battle prejudices and biases.

Overcoming Challenges:

1. Build self-esteem: Cultivate a strong feeling of self-worth and confidence in your talents. Surround yourself with helpful friends who celebrate your unique abilities and ideas, and separate yourself from bad influences that propagate damaging stereotypes.

2. Seek mentorship and support: Connect with mentors or role models who have had similar issues and can provide insight, encouragement, and solutions for handling barriers. Join support groups or communities that provide a safe and inclusive atmosphere.

3. Advocate for yourself: Don't be afraid to stand up and advocate for yourself when faced with stereotyping, discrimination, or unjust treatment. Communicate your concerns respectfully and seek support from appropriate resources or authorities when necessary.

4. **Cultivate resilience**: Develop a robust mindset that permits you to persevere in the face of hardship. Recognize that problems and failures are transient, and focus on your long-term goals and personal progress.

5. **Embrace your distinct identity**: Celebrate your cultural history, identity, and life experiences as sources of strength and uniqueness. Share your opinions and stories with others to develop an understanding and appreciation for diversity.

By actively trying to overcome challenges and preconceptions, you not only empower yourself but also contribute to establishing a more inclusive and equal society for everybody.

Celebrating Diverse Backgrounds and Perspectives

Diversity comprises a wide range of qualities, including color, ethnicity, gender, age, religion, sexual orientation, financial level, and physical or mental abilities. Embracing and honoring other backgrounds and opinions may enhance our lives, widen our understanding, and build a more inclusive and equitable society.

Benefits of Diversity:

1. Creativity and innovation: Diverse perspectives and experiences can lead to more creative and inventive solutions by bringing together unique opinions and ways of problem-solving.

2. Personal growth and understanding: Exposure to diverse cultures, beliefs, and experiences can extend our knowledge, challenge our assumptions, and foster personal growth and empathy.

3. Stronger teams and organizations: various teams and organizations can better reflect and fulfill the demands of various consumers, clients, or stakeholders, leading to enhanced decision-making, increased productivity, and superior overall performance.

4. Richer communities and societies: Embracing diversity contributes to the formation of vibrant, inclusive, and culturally rich communities and societies, where individuals from all origins can thrive and offer their unique talents and viewpoints.

Celebrating Diversity:

1. Learn about multiple cultures and identities: Seek opportunities to learn about and understand the history, traditions, and experiences of diverse communities. Attend cultural events, read literature, or engage in respectful debates to increase your understanding.

2. Embrace open and respectful communication: Foster a climate of open and courteous communication where individuals feel comfortable sharing their ideas, experiences, and concerns without fear of judgment or prejudice.

3. Recognize and confront biases: Be conscious of your personal biases and actively seek to challenge and overcome them. Encourage others to do the same by establishing safe spaces for uncomfortable conversations and encouraging inclusivity.

4. Promote varied representation: Advocate for diverse representation in numerous sectors, including media, leadership roles, and decision-making processes. Amplify the voices and stories of underrepresented or underprivileged communities.

5. Celebrate diversity through events and initiatives: Organize or participate in events, festivals, or initiatives that celebrate diversity and encourage cross-cultural understanding and appreciation. These can include cultural exhibitions, guest speakers, or community engagement initiatives.

By recognizing varied backgrounds and perspectives, we can create a more inclusive and equitable society where everyone feels valued, respected, and empowered to contribute their unique abilities and experiences.

Creating an Inclusive Career Plan

Developing an inclusive career plan is vital for ensuring that individuals from varied backgrounds and identities have equal opportunities to pursue their objectives and realize their full potential. By recognizing the specific difficulties and views of other groups, you may create a more equal and supportive atmosphere for everybody.

Assessing Personal Circumstances:
1. Identify potential hurdles: Reflect on your circumstances, background, and identity, and explore any potential barriers or challenges you may have in following your intended professional path. These could be budgetary limits, structural biases, or lack of representation in specific sectors.

2. Seek help and resources: Research and locate support networks, mentorship programs, scholarships, or groups that cater to individuals from your specific background or identity. These resources can provide direction, networking opportunities, and access to useful information and resources.

3. Develop strategies to overcome issues: Based on your assessment, develop proactive methods to address potential impediments or challenges. This could mean acquiring further training or education, creating a strong professional network, or pushing for inclusive policies and practices within your desired industry or workplace.

Creating an Inclusive Plan:

1. Set inclusive goals: Establish career goals that correspond with your values, interests, and personal circumstances, while also considering the possible impact of your aspirations on encouraging diversity and inclusion within your chosen area or business.

2. **Identify role models and mentors**: Seek out role models and mentors from varied backgrounds who have successfully navigated comparable career trajectories. Their experiences and ideas can provide significant direction and inspiration.

3. **Explore inclusive organizations and enterprises**: Research organizations, companies, or industries that value diversity, equity, and

inclusion in their practices and policies. These workplaces can offer more supportive and inclusive work cultures for persons from varied backgrounds.

4. Develop a strong personal brand: Cultivate a strong personal brand that welcomes and promotes your unique identity, experiences, and viewpoints. This can help you stand out and contribute to developing more diverse and inclusive workplaces.

5. Advocate for change: Be prepared to advocate for inclusive policies, practices, and opportunities within your desired job sector or workplace. Share your experiences and ideas to increase understanding and drive good change.

6. Embrace lifelong learning: Commit to continual learning and remaining updated about diversity, equity, and inclusion programs, best practices, and shifting societal trends. This knowledge can help you navigate and prosper in an ever-changing professional landscape.

By designing an inclusive career plan, you not only boost your chances of reaching your own goals but also help to foster a more varied, equitable, and inclusive society where everyone has the opportunity to achieve and reach their full potential.

Chapter Ten

Lifelong Learning and Adaptability

In today's fast-changing world, the capacity to embrace lifelong learning and adaptation is more vital than ever. The occupations of the future will demand individuals to consistently learn new knowledge, skills, and mindsets to be relevant and competitive. This chapter will discuss the value of establishing a growth mindset, engaging in continual learning and skill development, and being open to pivoting and recreating one's career path.

Developing a Growth Mindset

A growth mindset is the concept that one's abilities and intelligence can be developed through dedication, hard work, and a willingness to learn from failures and disappointments. Embracing this perspective is vital for personal and professional progress, as it encourages individuals to accept challenges, regard mistakes as chances for growth, and persist in the face of adversity.

The Power of Yet: One of the major elements of a development mindset is the concept of "not yet." Instead of perceiving failures or challenges as permanent limitations, persons with a growth mindset understand that they just haven't mastered a certain skill or concept yet. This mindset inspires tenacity and a dedication to ongoing progress.

Embracing difficulties: Individuals with a fixed attitude frequently shy away from difficulties, fearing failure or a perceived lack of skill. In contrast, persons with a growth mindset actively seek out problems as opportunities to stretch themselves, learn new things, and expand their capabilities.

Cultivating Grit: Grit, the mix of passion and tenacity, is a critical component of a growth mentality. Individuals with grit possess the tenacity and resilience to push through barriers and disappointments, realizing that true growth and achievement frequently involve prolonged work and a willingness to accept struggle.

Strategies for Developing a Growth Mindset:
- Recognize and reframe negative self-talk: Challenge fixed mindset notions like "I'm not good at this" and replace them with growth-oriented statements like "I can improve with practice."
- Embrace feedback as a gift: Seek out constructive criticism and consider it as a chance to uncover areas for growth and improvement.
- Celebrate work and progress: Focus on recognizing and appreciating the effort put forth, rather than just fixating on outcomes or results.
- Surround yourself with a growth-oriented environment: Seek out role models, mentors, and

peers who reflect a growth mindset and can inspire and support your journey.

By establishing a growth mindset, teens can acquire the resilience, determination, and love for learning that will serve them well throughout their jobs and personal lives.

Continuous Learning and Skill Development

In an era of rapid technology breakthroughs and increasing labor demands, ongoing learning and skill development are vital for staying competitive and adaptive in one's job. Embracing a lifelong learning mentality helps individuals to proactively upskill, reskill, and remain relevant in their chosen areas or explore other opportunities.

The Importance of Continuous Learning:

- **Future-proofing your career**: As sectors and work needs grow, ongoing learning ensures that your knowledge and abilities remain current and valuable.

- **Staying competitive**: In an increasingly global and competitive work market, people who consistently engage in their professional growth stand out and have a competitive edge.

- **Personal and intellectual growth**: Learning new skills and knowledge may be deeply gratifying, stimulating personal growth, intellectual curiosity, and a sense of accomplishment.

Strategies for Continuous Learning and Skill Development:

- **Formal education**: Consider obtaining further certificates, degrees, or specialized training programs to improve your knowledge or explore new areas of interest.

- **Online courses and self-study**: Leverage the enormous diversity of online learning platforms, tutorials, and educational materials to acquire new skills or extend your knowledge in a self-paced and flexible manner.

- **Attending workshops, conferences, and seminars**: Participate in industry events, workshops, and seminars to remain up-to-date with developing trends, network with professionals, and get useful insights.

- **Mentorship and work shadowing**: Seek out mentors or opportunities to job shadow established professionals in your desired sector to learn from their expertise and obtain hands-on experience.

- **Reading and research**: Stay informed by reading industry publications, books, and research papers to expand your understanding of your profession and explore new ideas.

- **Learning from experiences**: Treat every problem, project, or assignment as an opportunity to learn and grow, reflecting on your accomplishments and failures to identify areas for progress.

Developing a Personal Learning Plan:

To effectively manage continuous learning and skill growth, it's necessary to design a tailored learning strategy. This plan should fit with your professional goals, hobbies, and learning preferences, and should be periodically evaluated and changed as your aspirations and the job market evolve.

Key components of a personal learning plan:
- Conducting a self-assessment: Identify your existing strengths, shortcomings, and opportunities for growth to define your learning priorities.
- Setting SMART learning goals: Define concrete, measurable, achievable, relevant, and time-bound learning objectives to guide your efforts.
- Exploring learning resources: Research and find acceptable learning resources, such as courses, books, podcasts, or mentorship opportunities, that correspond with your goals.
- Creating a timeline and accountability system: Establish a realistic timeline and accountability measures, such as sharing your goals with a mentor or joining a study group, to keep on track.

- Reflecting and adjusting: Regularly examine your progress, celebrate victories, and alter your plan as needed to adapt to changing circumstances or emerging interests.

By adopting continual learning and skill development, youth may future-proof their professions, stay competitive, and uncover new prospects for personal and professional advancement.

Pivoting and Reinventing Your Career

In today's dynamic and ever-changing employment environment, the capacity to pivot and reconfigure one's career path is becoming increasingly valuable. Whether driven by personal growth, changing interests, or increasing industry demands, being open to career transitions can open up new prospects for fulfillment, success, and personal progress.

Understanding Career Pivots:

A career pivot refers to a dramatic adjustment or movement in one's professional course. This can require shifting to a new industry, career, or area completely, or it can mean investigating a different facet or specialism within the same sector. Career pivots can be proactive, driven by personal aspirations and goals, or reactive, spurred by external causes such as industry disruptions, job losses, or changing market demands.

Reasons for Pivoting and Reinventing Your Career:

- **Changing interests and passions**: As individuals grow and mature, their interests and passions may shift, leading them to pursue new paths that better correspond with their values and fulfillment.

- **Seeking work-life balance**: A professional pivot might provide an opportunity to establish a better work-life balance, explore flexible or remote work possibilities, or prioritize personal or family responsibilities.

- **Escaping a toxic work environment**: If an individual finds themselves in an unpleasant or unfulfilling work environment, a career pivot might offer a fresh start and an opportunity to prioritize personal well-being.

- **Exploring entrepreneurial projects**: Some individuals may opt to pivot from regular work to pursue entrepreneurial opportunities, leveraging their skills and expertise to develop their business enterprises.

- **Adapting to industry changes**: As sectors advance and particular professions or talents become obsolete, proactive individuals may pivot to stay relevant and capitalize on emerging opportunities.

Strategies for Successful Career Pivots:

- **Self-reflection and goal-setting**: Engage in deep self-reflection to discover your values, strengths, interests, and preferred lifestyle, and set clear goals for your career pivot.

- **Talent evaluation and transferability**: Analyze your existing skills and discover transferable talents that can be exploited in your chosen new sector or business.

- **Upskilling and reskilling**: Invest in learning new knowledge, certificates, or training programs to bridge any skill gaps and position yourself as a competitive candidate in your goal field.

- **Networking and informational interviews**: Connect with professionals in your target industry, conduct informational interviews, and tap into your network to gain insights, guidance, and potential opportunities.

- **Building a strong personal brand**: Craft a compelling personal brand that showcases your unique value proposition, experiences, and transferable abilities to stand out in your job search or entrepreneurial activities.

- **Developing a transition plan**: Create a detailed plan that details your career pivot goals, methods, timelines, and potential problems or impediments to resolve.
- **Embracing a growth attitude**: Approach your career pivot with an open and growth-oriented perspective, realizing that change and adaptability are vital for personal and professional growth.

While pivoting and recreating one's career can be tough, it can also be a wonderful and meaningful path of self-discovery, personal growth, and the quest for greater happiness and alignment with one's beliefs and objectives. By embracing adaptability and a willingness to explore new avenues, youth can position themselves for long-term career success and fulfillment in an ever-changing job landscape.

Exclusive Bonus

20 of the most profitable occupations in the digital era

In the digital age, various employment options have evolved, giving rich chances for individuals with the necessary skills and competence. Here are 20 of the most profitable occupations in the digital era:

1. Cybersecurity Specialist: With the rising reliance on digital technologies and the ever-present threat of cyber assaults, cybersecurity professionals are in great demand. They secure computer systems, networks, and data against illegal access, assuring the security and integrity of sensitive information.

2. Data Scientist: The ability to collect, analyze, and comprehend large amounts of data is important in today's data-driven environment. Data scientists utilize advanced statistical and computational approaches to extract insights, discover patterns, and inform strategic decision-making across many industries.

3. Artificial Intelligence (AI) and Machine Learning Engineer: As AI continues to change industries, specialists in this sector are increasingly sought after. They design and refine algorithms, neural networks, and machine learning models to automate processes, enhance decision-making, and drive innovation.

4. Software Developer: From smartphone applications to enterprise software solutions, software developers are the architects of the digital tools and platforms that fuel modern enterprises. With high demand and generous wages, this career offers several chances for specialization and growth.

5. Cloud Architect: As more firms shift their operations to the cloud, cloud architects play a critical role in developing, implementing, and maintaining cloud computing solutions. Their experience provides effective, scalable, and secure cloud infrastructures.

6. User Experience (UX) Designer: In a world where digital products and services are abundant, UX designers develop intuitive and engaging user experiences that drive consumer pleasure and loyalty. Their skills are highly recognized across numerous businesses, from technology to e-commerce.

7. Digital Marketing Specialist: With the advent of online platforms and social media, digital marketing specialists are vital for promoting businesses, engaging with customers, and increasing revenue through focused campaigns and data-driven initiatives.

8. Blockchain Developer: As blockchain technology continues to disrupt industries such as finance, supply chain, and healthcare, talented blockchain developers are in high demand. They design, construct, and maintain secure and decentralized blockchain-based applications and systems.

9. Mobile App Developer: With the proliferation of smartphones and tablets, mobile app developers produce unique programs that cater to many requirements, from entertainment and productivity to e-commerce and healthcare.

10. Virtual Reality (VR) and Augmented Reality (AR) Developer: The immersive experiences afforded by VR and AR technologies have applications in gaming, education, healthcare, and beyond. Developers adept in designing interesting VR and AR applications are widely sought after.

11. Ethical Hacker (Penetration Tester): As cybersecurity threats persist, ethical hackers, also known as penetration testers, play a key role in detecting and eliminating vulnerabilities in computer systems and networks, helping firms strengthen their defenses.

12. Social Media Manager: With the increased usage of social media platforms, organizations demand skilled social media managers to develop and execute effective social media strategies, engage with audiences, and drive brand awareness and customer loyalty.

13. Search Engine Optimization (SEO) Specialist: In the digital arena, visibility is vital. SEO consultants optimize websites and online content to boost search engine results, drive organic traffic, and increase online presence for organizations.

14. E-commerce Specialist: As more customers resort to online purchasing, e-commerce specialists are vital for designing and managing successful e-commerce platforms, optimizing user experiences, and increasing sales through efficient digital marketing techniques.

15. Web Developer: Web developers are responsible for designing and maintaining websites, ensuring they are user-friendly, visually appealing, and optimized for various devices and platforms.

16. Game Developer: The gaming business continues to flourish, and skilled game developers are in high demand. They develop immersive gaming experiences, combining cutting-edge technologies and storytelling strategies to attract audiences.

17. Digital Content Creator: From bloggers and vloggers to social media influencers, digital content creators can connect and engage with huge online audiences. Their ingenuity and skill to produce captivating material can lead to profitable opportunities through sponsorships, merchandise sales, and more.

18. IT Project Manager: In the digital age, IT projects are vital for driving innovation and company change. IT project managers oversee the design, execution, and effective delivery of technology-related projects, ensuring they are finished on schedule, within budget, and to the necessary specifications.

19. Business Intelligence Analyst: As organizations attempt to make data-driven decisions, business intelligence analysts play a critical role in obtaining, analyzing, and interpreting data to provide actionable insights and suggestions for strategic decision-making.

20. Cybersecurity Consultant: With the rising complexity of cyber threats, companies seek the experience of cybersecurity consultants to analyze their security posture, discover vulnerabilities, and develop effective security procedures to protect their digital assets and data.

These are just a few examples of the most profitable jobs in the digital age. As technology continues to advance, new opportunities will emerge, requiring individuals to be adaptable, embrace lifelong learning, and consistently upgrade their abilities to remain competitive in the changing digital economy.